AF413181

WHAT TO DO BEFORE, DURING AND AFTER A TORNADO

WEATHER BOOK FOR KIDS

CHILDREN'S WEATHER BOOKS

Speedy Publishing LLC

40 E. Main St. #1156

Newark, DE 19711

www.speedypublishing.com

Copyright 2017

In this book, we're going to talk about what to do before, during, and after a tornado. So, let's get right to it!

WHAT IS A TORNADO?

A tornado is a mass of swirling air. It's very fast and extends from the clouds in a thunderstorm to the surface of the Earth. In general, it's visible as a cloud that is shaped like a funnel. When a thunderstorm has both lightning as well as hail, there is a possibility that a tornado will be produced.

SPEED
LIMIT
75

Tornadoes around the world cause destruction to people, animals, land, and structures. They cause disruptions in all types of services, such as transportation, utilities, water sources, and communication. The thunderstorms surrounding a tornado can also cause extensive damage and heavy flooding.

Over 1,000 tornadoes form in the United States every year. About 60 people die annually from debris that is flying at fast speed when a tornado hits the ground.

Most of the tornadoes in the US are concentrated in the central as well as the southern plains. Very few tornadoes occur west of the Rocky Mountains. The Gulf Coast region and the state of Florida are areas that are also very susceptible to tornadoes.

Tornadoes usually happen in the months of spring and summer. They can happen at any time, but it's common for them to occur between the hours of 3 p.m. in the afternoon and 9 p.m. at night.

WHAT TO DO BEFORE A TORNADO STRIKES

If you live in an area that is prone to tornadoes, you should plan in advance so you will be able to act quickly. Tornadoes sometimes strike with little warning.

IDENTIFY SAFE PLACES IN ADVANCE

Make sure that you have identified safe places to go ahead of time. In order to withstand the strength of a tornado, a room must be built to quality standards that are designated by FEMA, which is the Federal Emergency Management Agency. Some storm shelters meet the construction standards of ICC 500. ICC stands for International Code Council.

TORNADO SHELTER

TORNADO SHELTER

In high-risk tornado areas, many people have a safe room shelter on their property. However, if you don't have a shelter, you'll need to find well-constructed buildings that meet these standards so you'll know where to travel if there is a tornado warning.

If you're in a building that has a roof with a long span, such as a mall or an educational institution, make sure you ask the building supervisor to share the storm plan with you in advance. Many people frequent these types of buildings so there must be an available plan in the event of a tornado.

MALL OF BERLIN
H&M
Taschen Paradies
KUSMI TEA

EMERGENCY KIT
GASOLINE

BUILD AN EMERGENCY KIT

You should have a basic emergency kit prepared ahead of time. You'll need one gallon of pure drinking water for each person for each day for a minimum of three days. You'll need a supply of canned or non-perishable food for at least three days for each person as well. A radio that's powered by batteries is important so you can stay tuned to weather alerts. Your kit should have a flashlight, first aid supplies, and extra batteries. A loud whistle is a good idea so you can call for help.

Dust masks are helpful as well since air is frequently contaminated after a tornado. Plastic sheeting and quality duct tape are supplies you should have in the kit in case you need to create a make-shift shelter. A pair of quality pliers to turn off the gas or other utilities is good to include. A can opener is needed if you are storing canned food. Maps of the local area and a cell phone with a backup battery as well as chargers are also useful.

Talk about where you would meet or what you would do if disaster strikes. Often, communication networks are down during a disaster so it's good to have a plan so you'll know where to find each other.

LISTEN TO THE RADIO

Listen to the radio or television reports from the NOAA, the National Oceanic and Atmospheric Administration. Pay attention and follow any instructions given by the officials in the local area.

BE ALERT TO THE WEATHER CONDITIONS

When you see a storm approaching, pay attention and get ready to move quickly if there is a tornado watch or warning. A tornado watch is sounded when tornadoes are likely to develop, which means you should be ready to travel to a safe room within a few minutes. A tornado warning signifies that a tornado has already been sighted by the weather bureau in your area. You should take shelter in a safe building or safe room immediately.

The sky is often dark and an eerie greenish color when tornado conditions exist. Large hail or rotating clouds that are close to the ground also signal a forming tornado. Loud roars that sound similar to a freight train mean that a tornado is very close. Be prepared to get into a shelter without delay.

DURING A TORNADO

If there is a tornado warning, don't wait, go into a safe shelter right away. Most people die during tornadoes because they are hit by flying debris, so be sure to protect your face and head from injury.

LARGE OCCUPANCY BUILDINGS

If you are in a large occupancy building like a school, a hospital, or a shopping area, go to the designated safe room if there is one. If a FEMA approved room isn't available, go to the lowest level possible and find a windowless room. Below ground is the best place to go if possible. Many people have survived tornadoes in a storm cellar or basement.

EXIT

Find a place with as many walls away from the outside wall as you can. Go under a well-built table and cover up your face, head, and neck with a heavy coat or pillows or a blanket. If you can, cover your arms and the rest of your body too. If you're in a high-rise building, go to a small inside room on the lowest possible level. Do NOT open the windows.

HOME OR OFFICE

If you have a safe room, go there. In tornado country, many people have basements or safe rooms somewhere on their properties. If you're in a mobile home, get out right away and go to a sturdy building. A tornado can easily pick up a mobile home and throw it around.

Simply Be Who You are
Don't worry be Happy!
HOME is where the HEART IS

OUTSIDE WITH NO SHELTER

Depending on where you are outdoors, there are many different actions you can take if you're in an area where a tornado hits. If you can get inside a vehicle, put your seat belt on, and drive away from the tornado to the nearest FEMA shelter.

When you're traveling, if your car or other vehicle is struck by debris, pull to the side of the road and park in a low-lying area if possible. Depending on how close the tornado is, you can take cover in a vehicle that is parked. Strap on the seat belt and wrap your head with a coat, blanket, cushion, or your arms.

NE HN 1562

Do NOT go underneath an overpass or under a bridge.
Low areas that are flat are better than these areas during
a tornado.

Do NOT try to speed faster than a tornado using a car or other vehicle if it's headed directly for you. It's best to abandon the vehicle and take cover in the closest sturdy building.

TORNADO IN CANADA

Staying outdoors is the worst thing you can do, because most people are killed by speeding airborne debris during a tornado.

AFTER A TORNADO

Don't try to move if you are trapped by debris. Strike a pipe or a nearby wall to make noise or if you have a whistle use it so that local rescuers can find you. If you are in your house or another building and are not trapped, listen to the radio for instructions. If possible, check in with your friends and family members by texting or calling. Be alert for falling debris and stay away from power lines that are down. Don't go into buildings that have sustained damage unless local officials say it's safe.

If there's a lot of heavy debris on your property, don't try to lift it or clean it up without help. When cleaning up outdoors wear quality protective clothing and heavy shoes so that you don't get scratched or step on something sharp.

Photograph any damage to your property so when the storm is over you can file for insurance or FEMA assistance. Do whatever you can to prevent additional damage to your home. For example, if there is a hole in the roof, cover it with a heavy tarp. Damage that happens once the storm is over is not always covered by insurance. If you don't have any power, use flashlights instead of candles, since candles are a fire hazard.

TORNADO CASUALTIES

SUMMARY

Tornadoes are dangerous, destructive storm clouds that are shaped like funnels and rotate at extremely high speed. Most people who die during tornadoes are hit by flying debris. You can survive a deadly tornado if you plan for what will happen before, during, and after the tornado.

Awesome! Now that you've read about what to do when a tornado strikes, you may want to read about how to perform some different weather experiments in the Baby Professor book Simulating Weather Experiments for Kids – Science Book of Experiments.

Visit

BABY PROFESSOR
EDUCATION KIDS

www.BabyProfessorBooks.com

to download Free Baby Professor eBooks
and view our catalog of new and exciting
Children's Books